W9-AGM-658

CRAFTY
Masks

Thomasina Smith

Gareth Stevens Publishing
MILWAUKEE

The original publishers would like to thank the following children, their parents, and Walnut Tree Walk Primary School for making this book possible: Charlie Anderson, Emily Askew, Chris Brown, Chan Chuvinh, Ngan Chuvinh, Isha Janneh, Sarah Kenna, Claire McCarthy, Imran Miah, and Marlon Stewart.

For a free color catalog describing Gareth Stevens' list of high-quality books and multimedia programs, call 1-800-542-2595 (USA) or 1-800-461-9120 (Canada). Gareth Stevens Publishing's Fax: (414) 225-0377.

Library of Congress Cataloging-in-Publication Data

Smith, Thomasina.
   Crafty masks / by Thomasina Smith.
     p. cm. — (Crafty kids)
   Includes bibliographical references and index.
   Summary: Provides instructions for making a variety of masks, including a Halloween witch, a wolf that turns into a lamb, and a bush spirit from Papua New Guinea.
   ISBN 0-8368-2482-2 (lib. bdg.)
   1. Mask making—Juvenile literature. 2. Masks—Juvenile literature.
[1. Mask making. 2. Masks. 3. Handicraft.] I. Title. II. Series.
TT898.S56   1999
745.59—dc21
                                      99-22876

This North American edition first published in 1999 by
Gareth Stevens Publishing
1555 North RiverCenter Drive, Suite 201
Milwaukee, WI 53212 USA

Original edition © 1996 by Anness Publishing Limited.
First published in 1996 by Lorenz Books, an imprint of Anness Publishing Inc., New York, New York.
This U.S. edition © 1999 by Gareth Stevens, Inc.
Additional end matter © 1999 by Gareth Stevens, Inc.

Editor: Sophie Warne
Photographer: John Freeman
Designer: Edward Kinsey
Gareth Stevens series editor: Dorothy L. Gibbs
Editorial assistant: Diane Laska

Printed in Mexico

1 2 3 4 5 6 7 8 9 03 02 01 00 99

Introduction

Masks have a long and fascinating history. Although their use and meaning have varied from culture to culture, masks have always transformed their wearers. Some were used for rituals and ceremonies in which the wearers were changed into gods and spirits. Others were used in the theater, in places such as Japan and ancient Greece.

Masquerade comes from the tradition of using masks at balls and festivals. At Carnival in Venice and Mardi Gras in New Orleans, thousands of people still parade the streets dressed up in fantastic masks.

The masks in this book are easy and fun to make. They use many different materials, from papier-mâché to everyday household objects. Masks have a variety of purposes: costume parties, theater productions, or even just decorations. So, make a mask and have fun wearing it!

Thomasina Smith

Contents

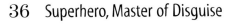

Materials

Although traditional masks are made of materials such as wood and clay, you can make masks from many other materials, too. Cardboard and papier-mâché are good basic materials, but, as you will see, you can also use items such as plastic ice cube trays, aluminum foil baking pans, woven baskets, and even autumn leaves. In fact, almost anything can be useful in mask-making. Start collecting odds and ends so you will never be short of materials.

KITCHEN STRAINERS

Stores that sell cooking equipment, including many hardware stores, usually have kitchen strainers in a range of sizes. These strainers are great for mask-making because you can see through them. Plastic strainers are better than metal ones; they come in bright colors and the mesh is made of white plastic, which is smoother and softer than woven strands of metal.

SWIMMING GOGGLES

If you do not already have swimming goggles, you can easily find them at sporting goods stores. Goggles are fun to use in a mask. They can also be an inexpensive substitute for safety glasses.

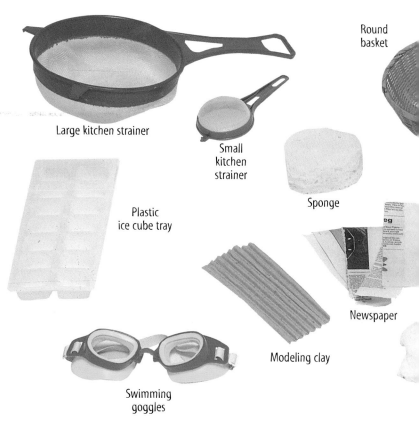

Large kitchen strainer

Round basket

Small kitchen strainer

Sponge

Plastic ice cube tray

Newspaper

Modeling clay

Swimming goggles

SPONGE

You can use a magic marker to draw any shape you want on an ordinary sponge. Cut the sponge with scissors.

COTTON

A roll of cotton is the best form to use for masks such as Santa Claus, but cotton comes in other forms, too.

PLASTIC FUNNEL

Plastic funnels make perfect noses for masks. They are available in hardware and kitchen supply stores.

SHOELACES

Why not paint some old shoelaces as a colorful alternative to elastic for tying on your masks?

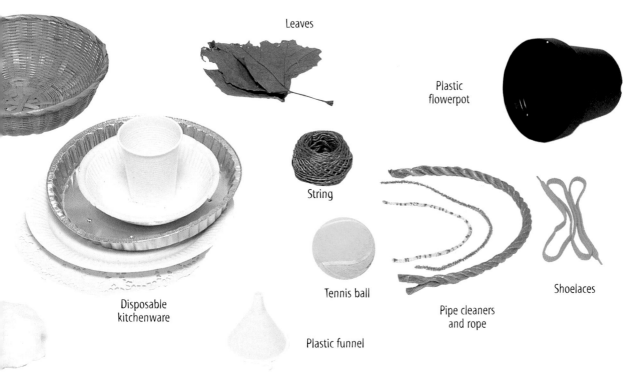

Leaves

Plastic flowerpot

String

Tennis ball

Pipe cleaners and rope

Shoelaces

Disposable kitchenware

Plastic funnel

Cotton

MODELING CLAY

You can make unusually shaped features for masks with modeling clay. They can be attached with glue and painted when dry.

LEAVES

Use leaves that are completely dry and handle them carefully.

TENNIS BALL

If you are making a large mask, such as the Spanish Giant, you can give it a great pair of eyes by cutting an old tennis ball in half. Cutting the ball can be tricky, so be sure to have an adult help you. You will need plenty of glue to attach these eyes. Then you can finish them with acrylic paints.

PIPE CLEANERS AND ROPE

You will find pipe cleaners — plain, colored, striped, or glittery — in many sizes and textures at art supply stores and craft shops. Thick rope can be unraveled or frayed to add hairy features, such as the beard on the Japanese Theater Mask.

Equipment

The equipment and tools needed for the masks in this book are easy to find in art supply, stationery, or hardware stores. Take care of your tools and try to keep them together in a box so you can easily find whatever you need.

ACRYLIC PAINTS

Acrylic paints are water-based, which means you can use water to clean your brushes and to dilute, or thin, the paint. Poster paints are a less expensive form of acrylic paints.

SPRAY PAINT

You can buy this paint in many colors at art supply stores, but car spray paint is a good alternative and costs less. Always wear a spray mask and spray only in well-ventilated areas.

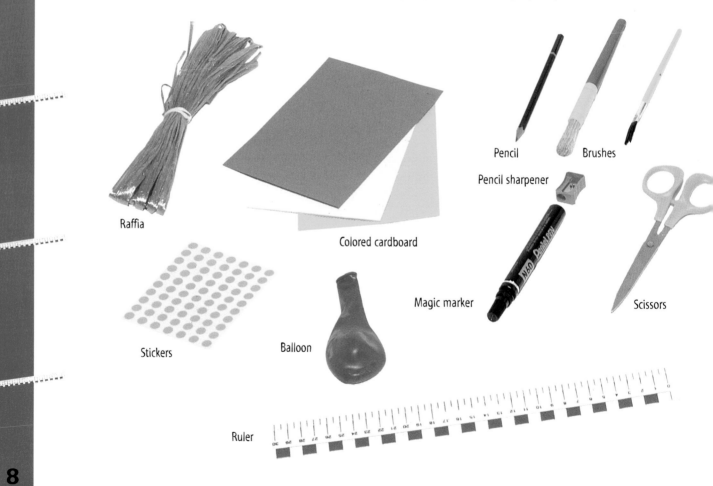

Raffia

Colored cardboard

Pencil

Brushes

Pencil sharpener

Stickers

Balloon

Magic marker

Scissors

Ruler

SPRAY MASK

When using spray paint, you should always wear a spray mask. These masks are available in most craft shops and hardware stores. A spray mask has a metal frame that holds a filter. The filter keeps tiny drops of paint from getting into your lungs when you breathe in. Spray mask filters should be changed frequently.

GLUE STICK

This form of glue is great for sticking a flat piece of paper to a smooth surface. Because a glue stick dries out quickly, always replace the lid.

WHITE GLUE

White glue, which is also known as wood glue, takes longer to dry than some glues, but it is very strong.

TAPE

You will need a variety of tapes for mask-making. Some colored tapes can be found in art supply stores, but hardware stores also have a good selection. Insulating tape or electrical tape is very strong, so it is great for holding things together. Masking tape is useful for holding things in place when you are gluing them together.

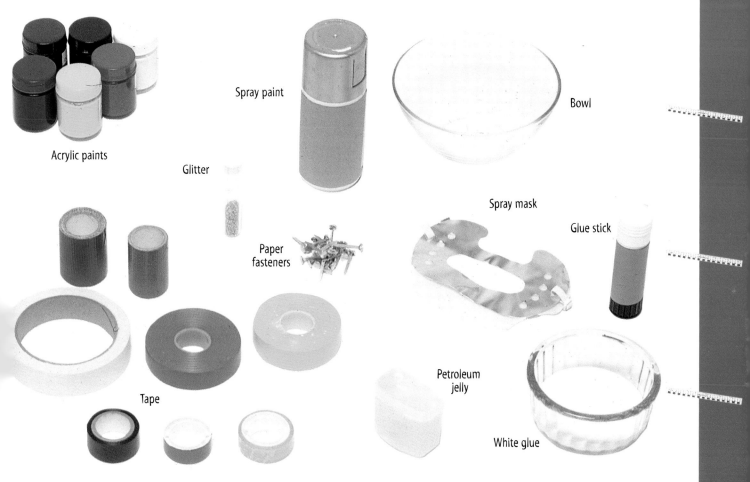

Acrylic paints

Spray paint

Bowl

Glitter

Paper fasteners

Spray mask

Glue stick

Tape

Petroleum jelly

White glue

Papier-Mâché

Some of the masks in this book are made with papier-mâché. Although traditional masks often use wood or clay as their base material, papier-mâché is a good substitute. You can mold it, and, when it is dry, it is hard and strong. Papier-mâché is made by soaking paper in a glue solution. There are several ways to make shapes with papier-mâché. One way is to build up layers of papier-mâché on a balloon. This technique is used to make the Spanish Giant mask. You could also cut this balloon shell in half and use each half to make a separate mask.

1 Make a glue solution by mixing together equal amounts of water and white glue. If you plan to make a lot of papier-mâché, use a bucket. Note that white glue is much stronger than wallpaper paste.

2 Tear or cut newspaper into strips and soak the strips in the glue solution.

3 Coat a balloon with petroleum jelly. You can use other types of molds, such as bowls, plates, and pans, to shape papier-mâché, but always coat them with petroleum jelly first so the papier-mâché is easy to remove when it is dry.

4 Apply layers of glue-soaked newspaper to the balloon. After each layer, coat the whole balloon with white glue for extra strength. Let each layer dry completely before you put on the next layer. You will usually need 3 or 4 layers.

5 When the papier-mâché is dry and solid, remove the mold. If the mold is a balloon, snip the bottom of the balloon with scissors to deflate it. Then remove the balloon.

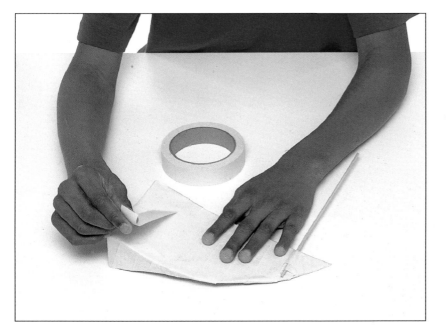

6 Another kind of mold, or base, for papier-mâché is a cardboard form, or shape. Cover the cardboard shape with masking tape, then apply layers of glue-soaked newspaper as in step 4. You do not have to use petroleum jelly with this kind of mold. When the final layer of papier-mâché is dry, remove the mask from the cardboard form.

Basic Techniques

FITTING A MASK

Before making a mask, it is a good idea to take measurements of your face; for example, the distance between your eyes and from your nose to your mouth, as well as the width around your head. You can draw around a pair of eyeglasses to mark the position of your eyes and the bridge of your nose. This measurement is especially useful for a project like the Venetian Mask.

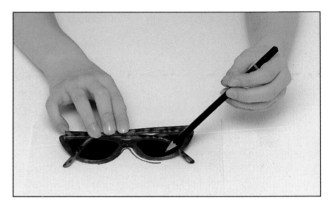

CUTTING EYE HOLES

1 Hold a paper plate or a piece of cardboard in front of your face. Use your fingers to carefully feel where your eyes are.

2 When you have found the exact locations of your eyes, mark the position of each eye on the paper plate with a pencil.

3 Draw two circles. Use closed scissors to poke a hole in the center of each circle. Then cut around the outline of each circle.

CUTTING A MOUTH

1 Draw a mouth on a paper plate. To be sure the mouth is even on both sides of the mask, cut it out by bending the plate in two and cutting across the fold.

SAFETY TIPS

1 When cutting any material that might fly up into your eyes, wear something to protect your eyes. You can get safety glasses from a hardware store, but swimming goggles are a good substitute.

2 When using spray paint, always wear a spray mask and work in a well-ventilated area. Remember to protect your work surface with scrap paper!

ATTACHING TIES AND STRAPS

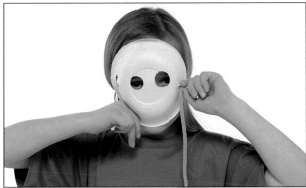

1 There are several ways to keep a mask on your head. Here is the easiest way. Cut two small slits on each side of the mask. Tie a strap through the slits on one side and fit the mask on your head. Bring the strap around the back of your head and pinch it at the length you need to reach the slits on the other side of the mask.

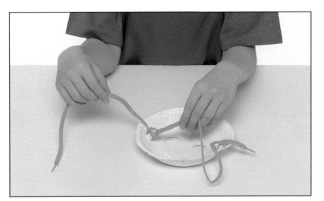

2 Keep holding the strap while you take the mask off and mark the place you are pinching with a pen. Then thread the free end of the strap through the slits on the other side of the mask and tie it firmly at the mark you just made on the strap. The mask should now fit your head and stay securely in place.

Basket Tiger

The idea for this mask is taken from traditional African masks, many of which looked like wild animals. The African masks were made from natural materials, such as clay and woven grasses.

YOU WILL NEED
- Round basket
- Scissors
- Orange cardboard
- Pencil
- Scrap of cardboard
- White glue and glue brush
- Acrylic paints and paintbrush
- Pipe cleaners
- String

1 Cut a round hole in the bottom of the basket with the scissors. If the basket is difficult to cut through, ask an adult to help you.

2 Place the basket on the orange cardboard and draw around the hole to make a circle for the tiger's face. Draw two ears at the top of the circle.

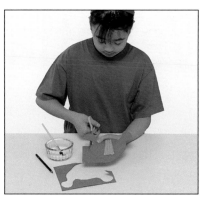

3 Cut out the face and ears. Then draw a nose on the scrap of cardboard, cut it out, and glue it on the face. When the glue is dry, cut out two eye holes.

4 Glue the face to the basket. When the glue is dry, paint the basket and the tiger's nose orange. Add features to the tiger's face with black paint, and glue on some pipe cleaners for whiskers.

5 Tie a piece of string to an opening in the basketwork on each side of the mask. Tie the mask securely around your head. Now, roar!

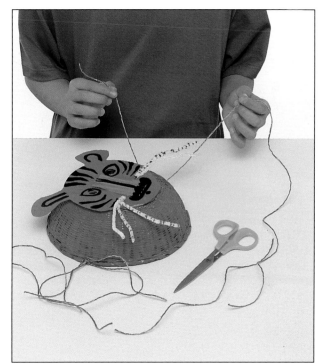

Venetian Mask

Venice is famous for its Carnival, when everyone dresses up in costumes and wears masks. Because this mask is on a stick, you don't have to wear it all the time. You can hold it in your hand like a fan.

YOU WILL NEED

- Pencil
- Cardboard
- Pair of glasses
- Scissors
- Glue stick
- Crepe paper
- Paper doily
- Wooden skewer or garden stick
- Glittery pipe cleaners
- White glue and glue brush

1 Draw the outline of the mask on cardboard, using a pair of glasses as a guide for the shape around your nose. Cut out the cardboard mask, including the eye holes.

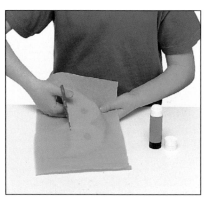

2 Cover the entire surface of the cardboard with glue and stick the crepe paper onto it. Trim the crepe paper from around the edges of the mask and the eye holes.

3 Fold the paper doily in half and cut out the circle in the center of it. Then cut the doily in half and fold one of the halves into pleats, like a fan.

4 Use the glue stick to attach the other half of the doily to the mask. Trim around the edges so the doily fits the cardboard shape.

5 Have an adult trim any sharp ends off the wooden skewer, then wind a glittery pipe cleaner around it. Attach the skewer to the back of the mask with white glue. Let the glue dry for at least an hour. Then glue the fan-shaped piece of the doily to the top of the mask. Cut a rectangle of crepe paper and wrap a pipe cleaner tightly around the middle of it to make a bow. Glue the bow onto the mask.

Golden Leaf Mask

Folk masks have been made and worn in Europe for hundreds of years. Some of these masks, in special Swiss festivals, for example, were made from leaves. Masks like the one shown here are still worn today!

YOU WILL NEED

- Circular aluminum foil baking pan
- Scissors
- White glue and glue brush
- Dry leaves (large and small)
- Gold spray paint
- Spray mask
- Old paper
- Wooden skewer or garden stick
- Pipe cleaner
- Thick electrical tape

1 With the scissors, carefully cut out the round bottom of the aluminum foil baking pan.

2 Brush white glue over the entire surface of this round piece of aluminum and cover the surface with dry leaves. Build up layers of leaves and allow the glue to dry thoroughly.

3 Protect your work surface with old paper, then spray the leaves with gold paint. Be sure you wear a spray mask and are working in an area that has plenty of fresh air. If you are inside, open a window.

4 Cut out two eye holes. Then, attach some small leaves to the wooden skewer with the pipe cleaner. Have an adult trim off any sharp ends. Spray the skewer and the leaves with gold paint. Glue the skewer to the back of the mask and secure it with thick electrical tape.

Crazy Specs

These crazy glasses are inspired by the ones you can find in joke shops. They will give you a truly unusual look!

YOU WILL NEED
- Black cardboard
- Pair of glasses
- Light-colored pencil
- Scissors
- Cardboard egg carton
- Acrylic paints and paintbrushes
- White glue and glue brush
- Masking tape
- Black pipe cleaners

1 Draw the outline of these goofy glasses on black cardboard with a light-colored pencil. Use a real pair of glasses as a guide to make the shape around your nose. Cut out the glasses with the scissors.

2 Cut two compartments out of the egg carton to make the eye pieces. Cut a hole in the center of each eye piece to see through. Then cut some cardboard from the lid of the egg box to make a silly nose. Paint the nose and the eye pieces.

3 When the paint is dry, glue the eyes and the nose onto the black cardboard glasses. While the glue is drying, it would be a good idea to prop the nose up against something and to use some masking tape to hold the nose in position.

4 Brush white glue on the ends of the cardboard glasses. Wrap a black pipe cleaner, over the glue, around each end. When the glue is completely dry, bend the pipe cleaners around your ears to keep your crazy specs in place.

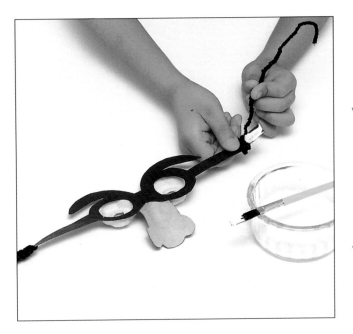

Wicked Witch

Make this wicked witch mask to disguise
yourself on Halloween. Just add
a broomstick to be on
your way!

YOU WILL NEED
- Paper plate
- Pencil
- Scissors
- Plastic funnel
- White glue and glue brush
- Green acrylic paint
- Paintbrush
- Red paper
- Black magic marker
- Raffia
- String
- Thick electrical tape
- Elastic

1 Draw a face on a paper plate and cut holes for the eyes. Place the plastic funnel in the center of the plate and draw around it. Cut out this circle, slightly inside the pencil line. Attach the funnel over the hole with white glue.

2 Paint the entire face green. Mix some white glue into the paint so it will stick to the funnel. Glue on a small circle of red paper to make a big wart. Color in the witch's facial features with a black magic marker.

3 To make the witch's scraggly hair, tie a big bunch of raffia together at one end with a piece of string. Use a piece of thick electrical tape to attach that end of the raffia to the top of the witch's head at the back of the mask.

4 Poke a hole in each side of the mask. Tie elastic through the hole on one side. Put the mask over your face, bring the elastic around the back of your head, and tie it through the hole on the other side.

23

Shining Skeleton

A skeleton is another perfect disguise to make for Halloween. This one is very spooky — it glows in the dark! Be sure to cut the eye holes big enough to see through clearly. Then close the curtains and turn off the lights!

YOU WILL NEED
- Light-colored pencil
- Black cardboard
- White cardboard
- Scissors
- Old paper
- Glow-in-the-dark paint
- Paintbrush
- White glue and glue brush
- Elastic

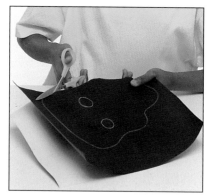

1 Draw a skeleton face on the black cardboard with a light-colored pencil. Hold the black cardboard and the white cardboard together while you cut out the face. When you cut out the eyes, be sure to cut through both layers of cardboard.

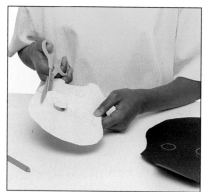

2 Trim around the edge of the white skeleton to make it slightly smaller than the black skeleton. Enlarge the eye sockets about ½ inch (1.3 centimeters). Cut out a nose and a mouth. Then cut the mouth off to make the jawbone.

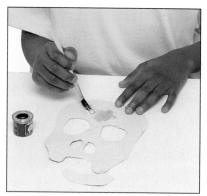

3 Protect your work surface with old paper, then coat the white skeleton with glow-in-the-dark paint. Read the instructions on the paint container carefully, and be sure to use the paint in an area that has plenty of fresh air.

4 When the paint is dry, glue the white skeleton face onto the black skeleton. Let the glue dry completely. Then poke a hole on each side of the mask, thread a piece of elastic through the holes, and tie the ends. You are ready for a haunting Halloween.

Santa Claus

Ho! Ho! Ho! See how easily some cardboard, a piece of red felt, and a roll of cotton can transform you into jolly old Santa Claus. This mask is perfect for the festive holiday season. Merry Christmas!

YOU WILL NEED
- Pencil
- Paper plate
- Red cardboard
- Ruler
- Scissors
- White glue and glue brush
- Red felt
- Cotton
- String

1 Draw around the paper plate to make the curved part of Santa's beard. Draw a mouth in the beard. Then draw a hat shape on red cardboard, with a band 32 inches (80 cm) long and 1½ inches (4 cm) wide at the bottom.

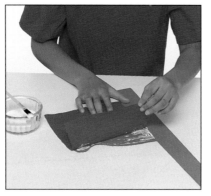

2 Cut out the beard and the hat shapes. Spread glue over the top part of the hat, but do not put glue on the band. Stick a piece of red felt over the glue. Do not stick felt onto the band of the hat. Let the glue dry thoroughly.

3 Trim around the edge of the hat shape with the scissors to remove the extra felt. Be very careful not to cut into or through the band of the hat when you are trimming the felt.

4 Spread white glue on the band of the hat and the beard and stick cotton to it. When the glue is dry, trim the cotton around the hat band and the top of the beard.

5 Attach a piece of string to each side of the beard and tie the string at the back of your head. Wrap the band of the hat around your head until it fits. Mark, with your finger, where the ends of the band meet. Glue the ends of the band together at that spot.

27

Easter Rabbit

When you make this rabbit mask, use sponges to give the bunny plump cheeks.

YOU WILL NEED
- Colored cardboard
- Pencil
- Scissors
- Two sponges
- Black magic marker
- Scrap of black paper
- Scrap of white paper
- Glue stick
- White glue and glue brush
- Six wooden skewers or garden sticks
- Pipe cleaners

1 Draw a rabbit face (with long ears), 12 inches (30 cm) wide and 24 inches (60 cm) high, on thin, colored cardboard. Cut out the face and cut two holes in it for the eyes.

2 Draw a round shape onto each of the two sponges with the black magic marker. Use scissors to cut these shapes out for the rabbit's cheeks.

3 Draw a mouth on the face with the magic marker. Cut a nose out of black paper and a pair of teeth out of white paper. Attach them both to the mask with a glue stick.

4 Use white glue to attach the rabbit's sponge cheeks. Let the glue dry completely. Then, dab a little glue onto one end of each wooden skewer. Insert three skewers into each sponge for the rabbit's whiskers. Have an adult trim the whiskers, if necessary, to remove any sharp ends.

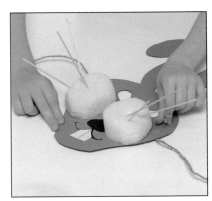

5 Poke a hole on each side of the mask. Thread a pipe cleaner through each hole and twist the end to hold it in place. To wear your rabbit mask, hook the pipe cleaners around your ears.

HANDY HINT

When you attach the sponges for the rabbit's cheeks, be sure to use plenty of white glue. The sponges will absorb a lot of it. Also, allow plenty of time for the glue to dry.

Hungry Wolf, Unlucky Lamb

This type of mask comes from the Pacific Northwest. It is called a transformation mask because it can change from one animal into another. This transformation mask tells the story of an unlucky lamb eaten by a hungry wolf.

YOU WILL NEED

- Two circular aluminum foil baking pans
- Black magic marker
- Plastic cup
- Scissors
- White glue and glue brush
- Acrylic paints and paintbrushes
- Black cardboard
- Red paper
- Glue stick
- Thick electrical tape
- Pair of shoelaces
- Elastic

1 Put one baking pan on top of the other. Use the black magic marker to draw around a plastic cup in the center of the top pan. Have an adult help you cut through both pans to make a hole for the nose in the center of this circle. Then cut holes for the eyes and mouth.

2 Separate the two baking pans and cut the top pan in half, straight down the center of the nose and between the eyes. Cutting aluminum foil baking pans could create sharp edges. Always have an adult help you to make sure the edges are smooth.

3 On one half of the baking pan that was cut in half, glue the plastic cup along the magic-marker line with white glue. Let the glue dry.

4 Paint both halves of the baking pan with the plastic cup nose to look like a wolf. Paint the other pan to look like a lamb. Mix white glue into the paint so the paint will stick to the aluminum. Cut two wolf ears out of black cardboard and paste a triangle of red paper on each one with the glue stick. Attach the wolf's ears to the mask with white glue.

5 Let the paint on both masks dry completely. Then, hinge the wolf mask to the lamb mask with four pieces of thick electrical tape. Tape hinges on both the inside and outside of the masks. The wolf mask should close over the lamb mask. Also use electrical tape to attach a shoelace to the inside edge of each half of the wolf mask. You will tie and untie the shoelaces to transform the mask. Poke a hole into each side of the finished mask for an elastic strap. Measure your head before tying the elastic to both sides of the mask.

31

Polar Bear

The secret to making a bear mask is to give it a really good snout. What could be better than a plastic flowerpot that has ready-made holes for you to breathe through? If you are not able to find a flowerpot, you can use a yogurt container and ask an adult to poke two holes in the bottom.

YOU WILL NEED

- Paper plate
- Pencil
- Scissors
- Ruler
- Fake fur
- White glue and glue brush
- Plastic flowerpot with a 5-inch (12.5-cm) diameter and at least 2 drainage holes
- Masking tape
- Pink fabric
- Colored electrical tape
- String

1 Draw a bear face with ears on the paper plate. Cut out eye holes. Then draw a rectangle, 3 inches (7.5 cm) long, underneath the face. Cut out the face and cut four slits into the bottom of the rectangle to make flaps. You will use these flaps later to attach the snout to the bear's face.

2 Cut a square of fake fur slightly bigger than the bear's face and glue it on. Then cut a fur rectangle 1 inch (2.5 cm) wider than the height of the flowerpot and a little longer than the measurement around the top edge of the pot. Cut 3-inch (7.5-cm) slits along one long edge of the rectangle with a 3-inch (7.5-cm) gap between slits.

3 Trim the fur around the bear's head. Wrap the fur rectangle around the flowerpot with the slits at the bottom. Brush white glue around the inside edge of the pot and fold the fur over the edge to stick it down inside. Glue the fur to the outside of the pot. (The flaps will overlap at the base of the pot.) Trim the fur around the base.

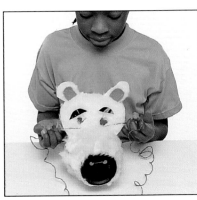

4 Glue the flaps on the face to the inside of the snout. Hold the snout in place with masking tape until the glue dries. Cut ear shapes out of pink fabric and glue them in place. Make eyebrows and a mouth out of colored electrical tape.

5 Cut out the eye holes again. Then thread a yard (meter) of string through two holes in the snout. Wrap the string around the top of the pot and tie it in a knot. Put the pot over your face and tie the strings behind your head.

Spanish Giant

Instead of covering your face, this mask sits on top of your head. Tulle netting falling from the mask disguises the wearer. Masks like this one are used in Spanish carnivals and are often two or three times the size of the people wearing them.

YOU WILL NEED

- Balloon
- Petroleum jelly
- Bowl
- Newspaper
- White glue and glue brush
- Acrylic paints and paintbrushes
- Scissors
- Tennis ball
- Masking tape
- Elastic
- Tulle netting
- Fake fur

1 Blow up a balloon and coat it with petroleum jelly. Then cover the balloon with several layers of papier-mâché. Let the papier-mâché dry until it is hard.

2 Snip the neck of the balloon with the scissors to let the air out, then pull the balloon skin out of the papier-mâché shell.

3 Ask an adult to cut a tennis ball in half for you. Glue the halves onto the papier-mâché shell for eyes. Hold them in place with masking tape until the glue dries.

4 Paint the mask. Use a thick paintbrush to apply the base coat and a thinner one to paint on the details.

HANDY HINT
When painting the face, make sure you leave enough space under the mouth to trim the base of the mask. It might be a good idea to make sure the mask fits before you paint it.

5 When the paint is dry, trim the base of the mask so it sits firmly on your head. Then make a hole in each side and tie elastic onto one side. Have someone hold the mask on top of your head while you fit the elastic under your chin and tie it to the other side. Tape 2 yards (2 m) of tulle netting around the base of the mask for a veil and glue on a fake fur collar.

35

Superhero, Master of Disguise

A comic strip superhero flies,
defeats evil, and always wears
a mask. Is it a bird?
Is it a plane?
No, it's Superhero!

YOU WILL NEED

- Scrap of cardboard
- Scissors
- Two small plastic strainers
- Clear tape
- Colored electrical tape
- Pair of tights
- Colored cardboard

1 To make goggles, cut a scrap of cardboard to 1 inch (2.5 cm) by ½ inch (1.3 cm) and stick it between the two plastic strainers with clear tape to form a bridge across the nose.

2 Cover the bridge with colored electrical tape. Then make a strap to go around the back of your head. Cut a strip of colored tape 2 feet (60 cm) long. Place another strip of tape the same length on top of the first, sticky side down. Tape one end of this strap to the goggles.

3 To make a helmet, cut one leg off of a pair of tights. Cut a hole halfway down the leg, making the hole large enough to fit around your face. Put the leg over your head, tie it at the top, and cut the foot off.

4 Decorate the top of the helmet with a symbol cut out of colored cardboard. Stick the symbol onto the helmet with colored tape. Make sure the goggles fit, then tape the loose end of the strap to the goggles.

HANDY HINT

Remember that tights are stretchy, so when you make the face hole in your tights, start by cutting a small hole and trying it on for size. Then, if necessary, make the hole bigger.

Sunshine

This colorful mask is very easy to make! You do not even have to make holes for the eyes or mouth. All you have to do is decorate it.

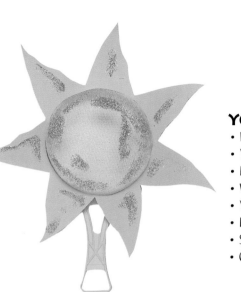

YOU WILL NEED
- Large plastic strainer
- Yellow acrylic paint
- Paintbrush
- White glue and glue brush
- Yellow cardboard
- Pencil
- Scissors
- Gold glitter

1 Paint the plastic strainer bright yellow. Mix white glue into the paint so the paint will stick to the plastic.

2 Center the strainer on the yellow cardboard. Draw around the circular part of the strainer and draw big sun rays coming out of the circle. Cut around the sun rays, then cut out the center of the circle, keeping the sun rays attached along the outside edge.

3 Brush patches of white glue onto the strainer and the sun rays. Sprinkle these patches with gold glitter and let the glue dry.

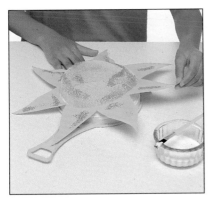

4 Brush some glue around the bottom edge of the strainer. Then push the circle of sun rays down over the mesh. Let the glue dry thoroughly before you hold the mask up in front of your face.

Coco the Clown

If you enjoy the circus, then you will love this mask. Use copper scouring pads to make this clown's wild hair.

YOU WILL NEED

- Two paper plates
- Pencil
- Scissors
- Acrylic paints and paintbrush
- Colored tape
- Raffia
- Plastic bottle cap
- White glue and glue brush
- Colored electrical tape
- Six copper scouring pads
- Paper fasteners
- Elastic

1 Cut two eye holes out of one of the paper plates. Paint on a cheerful clown face and let the paint dry.

2 Draw a triangular hat and a bow tie on the other paper plate and cut them out. Paint the bow tie and decorate the hat with colored tape and raffia.

3 Use the plastic bottle cap for the clown's nose. Paint it with a mixture of white glue and red paint.

4 Glue the hat to the back of the mask and secure it with electrical tape. Attach the copper scouring pads to the top of the mask, using paper fasteners to hold them in place. Glue the bow tie to the front of the mask below the mouth. Cut a hole in each side of the mask. Tie elastic on one side, then fit the elastic around your head and tie it to the other side.

Greek Tragedy Mask

Actors in ancient Greece used masks with both comic and tragic expressions. Today, a comedy and a tragedy mask are often shown together to symbolize the theater.

YOU WILL NEED
- Paper plate
- Pencil
- Scissors
- Modeling clay
- White glue and glue brush
- Old paper
- Gold spray paint
- Spray mask
- Black acrylic paint
- Paintbrush
- Wide ribbon

1 Draw the outline of a tragic face on the paper plate and cut it out. Then cut holes for the eyes and the mouth, making them look as sad as possible.

2 Mold a piece of modeling clay into a triangular shape for the nose. Glue it onto the paper plate with plenty of white glue. Sculpt the clay so the edges of the nose are smooth against the plate. Coat the clay nose with glue and let it dry.

3 Place the mask on some old paper and spray it with gold paint. Remember to wear a spray mask. Wait a few minutes for the paint to dry.

DON'T FORGET!

Use spray paint only in a place that has plenty of fresh air. If you are inside, open a window. Always wear a spray mask, which you can buy at a hardware store or a craft shop. Be sure to lay down enough old paper to protect your work area, and avoid places like a brand new carpet or the dining room table!

4 Outline the eyes, mouth, and nose with black paint and add lines of black paint for the chin, cheeks, and eyebrows.

5 Cut two long pieces of wide ribbon and attach one to each side of the mask, at the back, with white glue. Let the glue dry completely before using the ribbons to tie on the mask.

Bush Spirit Mask

Bush spirit masks come from Papua New Guinea. They are made for ceremonies that celebrate the bush spirits, or Kovave. This simple version of a bush spirit mask is made from cardboard and fabric. The fringe at the bottom of the mask covers the wearer's shoulders to give the effect of a bird's body.

YOU WILL NEED
- Corrugated cardboard
- Ruler
- Pencil
- Scissors
- Masking tape
- White glue and glue brush
- Rubber or plastic faucet nozzle
- Acrylic paints and paintbrushes
- Two pieces of bow-tie pasta
- Fabric
- Electrical tape
- String

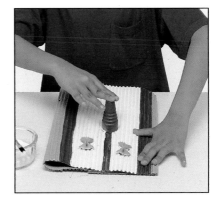

1 Cut the cardboard into a large square measuring 28 inches (70 cm) on each side. Fit the cardboard around your head and hold it in a tube shape with masking tape.

2 Glue the seam of the tube where the edges overlap. When the glue is dry, remove the masking tape. Paint the rubber nozzle brown. Add some white glue to the paint so the paint will stick to the rubber. Paint brown stripes on the mask and paint the spaces between them white.

3 Use white glue to stick the rubber nozzle onto the cardboard, between the stripes, for a nose. Glue the two bow-tie pasta pieces on for eyes. Let the glue dry.

4 Cut a piece of fabric, 24 inches (60 cm) by 36 inches (90 cm), into strips 1 inch (2.5 cm) wide. Attach the strips to a long piece of electrical tape to make fringe a yard (meter) long. Attach the fringe inside the bottom edge of the mask with white glue. Let the glue dry.

5 Poke two holes on each side of the mask. Tie a piece of string through the holes on each side. To wear the mask, put it on your head and tie the strings together under your chin.

Crocodile

There is a long tradition in mask-making of using everyday materials from around the home. With this crocodile mask, an ice cube tray takes on a new life!

YOU WILL NEED

- Thin cardboard
- Ruler
- Pencil
- Scissors
- Plastic ice cube tray
- White glue and glue brush
- Masking tape
- Two pieces of bow-tie pasta
- Acrylic paint and paintbrushes
- Colored dot stickers
- White fabric tape

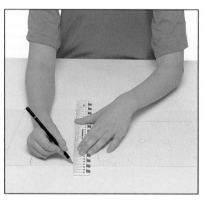

1 For the crocodile's face, draw an 8-inch (20-cm) square, with a zigzag line down the two side edges. Draw two circles on the face for eye holes. For the crocodile's snout, draw around the ice cube tray twice on cardboard. Draw flaps around each rectangle; one rectangle will need a flap, on each long side, that is wider at one end. Cut around the outlines, leaving the tabs for gluing the crocodile's snout together.

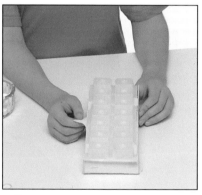

2 Cut out the eye holes and cut two slits below the outside edge of each eye for a fabric-tape tie. Use scissors to score along the lines of the snout flaps. Be sure to move the scissors away from you. Fold and glue the tabs, holding the corners in place with masking tape until the glue dries. Glue the ice cube tray facedown on the top of the snout. Use masking tape to hold it in place. Glue the snout to the face.

3 Glue a piece of bow-tie pasta above each eye for eyebrows. Paint the crocodile's face and the top of its snout blue. Paint teeth on the sides of the snout. When the paint is dry, add colored dot stickers.

4 Thread the white fabric tape through the slits next to the eyes. The tape will show at the front of the mask, so decorate it with a line of dot stickers. To wear the mask, tie the ends of the fabric tape behind your head.

Talking House

Not all masks are faces or animals. Masks can also create the illusion of a talking house or a dancing teapot (see page 56). To make a matching costume for this talking house mask, you could dress all in green. Then your house would be the house on the hill!

YOU WILL NEED
- Cardboard
- Ruler
- Pencil
- Scissors
- Acrylic paints and paintbrushes
- White glue and glue brush
- Cotton
- Ribbon

1 Draw a house, 10 inches (25 cm) by 12 inches (30 cm), on a piece of cardboard. Draw on two eye holes and a hole for your nose. Don't forget to add a puff of smoke coming out of the chimney!

2 Cut out the house shape. Then cut out the holes for the eyes and the nose.

3 Paint the house red. When the red paint is dry, paint on some bricks with yellow paint. Then paint some windows, a door, and other details on the roof and chimney with black paint.

4 Brush white glue over the smoke shape and stick some cotton to it. Then dab gray paint onto the cotton to make it look like smoke. If you do not have any gray paint, you can make some by mixing black and white paints together.

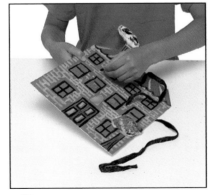

5 Make two holes in the house that line up with each side of your head. Start at the back of the mask and thread the ribbon through the holes. The ribbon will pass across the front of the mask, so choose a color that blends in.

HANDY HINT

You could add a tree on the front of your talking house mask. Draw a tree shape with black acrylic paint. Brush white glue over the treetop and stick some cotton to it. Then dab green paint onto the cotton treetop.

Beaky Bird

This clever mask has a beak that moves up and down. The idea came from a ceremonial mask of the Pacific Northwest.

YOU WILL NEED
- Thin white cardboard
- Pencil
- Ruler
- Scissors
- White glue and glue brush
- Masking tape
- Newspaper
- Bowl
- Wooden skewer or garden stick
- Acrylic paints and paintbrushes
- Colored cardboard
- Electrical tape
- Elastic

1 Draw the mask pieces on thin cardboard. The face should be an oval about 12 inches (30 cm) by 4 inches (10 cm). For the upper beak, you will need two pieces of cardboard, each about 1½ inches (3.8 cm) wide by 6 inches (15 cm) long. You will also need two pieces for the lower beak, each about 6 inches (15 cm) long and 3 inches (7.5 cm) deep. Cut out all the pieces.

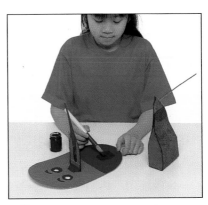

2️⃣ Use a pair of scissors to score a flap along the straight edge of each piece of the upper and lower beak. Remember to move the scissors away from you. Bend the flaps of the beak.

3️⃣ Use the flaps to glue together the two lower beak pieces and one of the upper beak pieces. Wrap masking tape around this form to make a solid box. Cover the beak form with two layers of papier-mâché, letting it dry between layers. Tape the skewer to the end of the lower beak. Add two more layers of papier-mâché.

4️⃣ Glue the flap of the remaining piece of the upper beak onto the face. When the glue is dry, paint the face and the upper beak.

5️⃣ Cut out a cardboard feather and glue it to the back of the mask. Hinge the lower beak to the face using two pieces of electrical tape at the bottom of it. Put one piece of tape on the outside of the beak, the other underneath it. Move the beak up and down with the skewer. Add an elastic strap to fit your head.

Fish Face

Masks can be made to look like almost anything — and they can be made from almost anything! Here, a pair of swimming goggles is used to make a mask of a fish swimming underwater through seaweed.

YOU WILL NEED

- Colored cardboard
- Pencil
- Scissors
- Swimming goggles
- Masking tape
- Glue stick
- Black magic marker

1 Draw a fish shape, 10 inches (25 cm) by 4 inches (10 cm), on colored cardboard and cut it out. Also draw and cut out a small eye and two pieces of curly seaweed.

2 Place the swimming goggles on the fish and draw around them. Hold the goggles in place with masking tape while you draw.

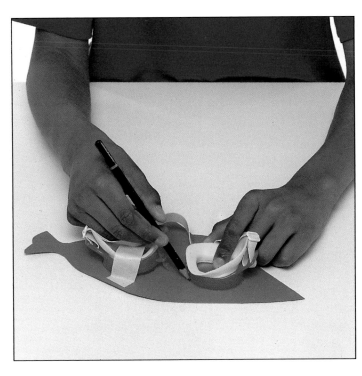

3 Cut out the eye holes. Then cut two small slits, one on the outside of each eye hole, for the strap of the goggles to pass through. Now, take the strap off the goggles.

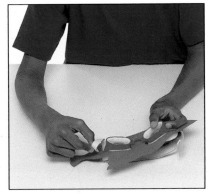

4 Push the goggles into the eye holes, then thread the strap back through the slits in both the goggles and the mask.

5 Decorate the fish by attaching the eye and the seaweed with a glue stick. Use black magic marker to draw in the details of the fish's scales and fins.

Happy and Sad Mask

Some masks have more than one expression. This mask has both a happy and a sad mouth. You could also make a mask that wakes and sleeps by having a pair of closed eyes on one stick and a pair of open eyes on another.

YOU WILL NEED
- Paper plate
- Scissors
- Acrylic paints and paintbrushes
- Pencil
- Cardboard
- Thin sponge
- Two wooden skewers or garden sticks
- White glue and glue brush
- Ribbon

1 Cut out eye holes in the paper plate. Check their position against your face before you start cutting. Paint one half of the plate yellow and the other half blue. When this paint is dry, use black paint to add all of the facial features except a mouth.

2 Draw a happy mouth and a sad mouth on cardboard and cut them out. Draw around them onto the thin sponge and cut out the sponge shapes. If the wooden skewers have sharp ends, have an adult remove them for you. Coat each cardboard mouth with white glue and sandwich a skewer between the cardboard and the sponge.

3 Glue a piece of ribbon about 1 yard (1 m) long onto the back of the mask, below the eye holes. Let the glue dry thoroughly before using the ribbon to tie on the mask. To wear the mask, tie the ribbons together in a bow at the back of your head.

4 Paint the sponge mouths with red acrylic paint. When the paint is completely dry, why not use the mouths to tell a happy and sad story?

DON'T FORGET!

Do not try to trim the sharp ends off of wooden skewers or garden sticks by yourself. Always have an adult help you.

Teapot

Here is a fun idea for a tea party — come disguised as a bright red, polka-dotted teapot! This mask calls for papier-mâché and finger paints.

YOU WILL NEED
- Circular aluminum foil baking pan
- Scissors
- Cardboard
- Pencil
- White glue and glue brush
- Paper fasteners
- Bowl
- Newspaper
- Red acrylic paint
- Paintbrush
- White finger paint
- Ribbon

1 Cut out eye and mouth holes in the aluminum foil baking pan. Check their position against your face before you start cutting. Watch out for sharp edges when you are cutting aluminum.

2 Draw the teapot's handle, lid, and spout on a piece of cardboard. To make sure they are the right size, draw around the baking pan on the cardboard and draw the handle, lid, and spout next to it.

3 Cut out the handle, lid, and spout and attach them to the baking pan with white glue and paper fasteners. When the glue is dry, apply papier-mâché over the glued areas and let it dry thoroughly.

4 Paint the teapot with red acrylic paint. When the red paint is dry, dot the entire mask, including the handle, lid, and spout, with spots of white finger paint.

5 Make two holes, about 1 inch (2.5 cm) apart, on each side of the mask at about eye level. Thread the ribbon through both holes on each side and knot it behind the holes to hold it in place. To wear the mask, tie both sets of ribbons together at the back of your head.

SAFETY AND COMFORT TIP

To make this mask safe and comfortable to wear, stick tape around the cut edges of the eye and mouth holes before you apply the papier-mâché.

Egyptian Mummy

In ancient Egypt, masks were used for burials. Rich and important people were mummified when they died, and beautiful masks of their faces were made for them to wear. The masks were made from wood and were decorated with gold. You can make this Egyptian mask without having to use real gold!

YOU WILL NEED

- Black cardboard
- Light-colored pencil
- Paper bowl
- Compass
- Ruler
- Scissors
- Colored electrical tape
- Acrylic paints and paintbrushes
- White glue and glue brush
- Elastic

1 Use a light-colored pencil to draw the shape of a mummy's head, about 10 inches (25 cm) by 16 inches (40 cm), on black cardboard. Draw around the paper bowl on the head shape to make the face. Use a compass to draw a circle inside the face, making it about ½ inch (1.3 cm) smaller. Draw a long, thin rectangle from this circle to the bottom of the mummy shape. Cut out the rectangle and the circle.

2 Decorate the black head shape with stripes of brightly colored electrical tape. Turquoise, red, and gold were popular colors with the ancient Egyptians.

3 Cut two eye holes in the bottom of the paper bowl. Paint the bowl yellow. When the yellow paint is dry, paint on the facial features in black.

4 Attach the paper bowl face onto the decorated head shape with plenty of white glue. When the glue is dry, poke two small holes into each side of the mask, thread elastic through them, and fit the mask onto your head.

59

Japanese Theater Mask

One of the most famous forms of traditional Japanese theater is called Noh. This mask is a copy of one of the characters in Noh theater. The Japanese made their masks with wood, but you can use papier-mâché.

YOU WILL NEED

- Corrugated cardboard
- Ruler
- Pencil
- Scissors
- Saucepan
- Petroleum jelly
- Masking tape
- White glue and glue brush
- Bowl
- Newspaper
- Acrylic paints and paintbrushes
- Thick rope

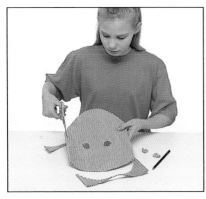

1 Cut a face shape, 12 inches (30 cm) by 10 inches (25 cm), out of corrugated cardboard. Draw on eyes and a mouth. Check their position against your face before cutting them out.

2 Coat the curved outside edge of the saucepan with petroleum jelly and use masking tape to attach the base of the mask to the saucepan. Apply two layers of papier-mâché to the surface of the mask. Let the first layer dry before adding the second. When both layers are dry, remove the mask from the saucepan and add a third layer of paper-mâché, folding the newspaper strips around the eye and mouth holes to make smooth edges.

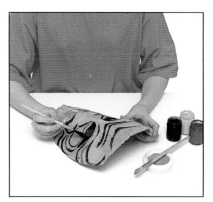

3 Mix red and yellow acrylic paints to make an earthy orange color and paint the mask with it. When the orange paint is dry, paint black lines onto the mask for the facial features.

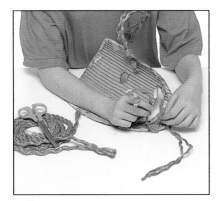

4 To make a beard, poke three holes in the chin of the mask. Fray the rope and tie two strands of it through each hole. Make a strap by poking a hole on each side of the mask and tying a piece of rope through each hole. The two pieces of rope should fit around your head.

Glossary

bush: a region, or large area of land, that is overgrown with stunted trees and scrublike plants and does not have many inhabitants.

ceremonial: related to the particular activities, rituals, and procedures that celebrate certain special occasions and events.

facial features: the individual parts of the face, such as eyes, eyebrows, nose, and mouth.

felt: (n) a thick, heavy fabric made by heating and pressing together, rather than weaving, wool and other fibers.

fray: to cause, usually by pulling or rubbing, the threads or fibers of cloth, or other woven materials, to weaken and separate.

fringe: threads, strands, or strips of material that hang down loosely from some kind of edging to form a decorative border.

hinge: (v) to attach a movable joint on which something moves up and down or swings open and closed.

illusion: an appearance or image that fools the senses into believing that something false is real.

Papua New Guinea: an independent nation in the South Pacific, just north of Australia, that includes a chain of tropical islands extending more than 1,000 miles (1,600 kilometers).

pleats: a series of evenly spaced flat folds in cloth or paper, made by doubling the material over onto itself and pressing the folds to make sharp, straight creases.

raffia: paperlike strands of fiber from the raffia palm, used in a variety of crafts, including weaving mats and baskets and making hats.

score: (v) to cut or scratch a shallow groove with a sharp instrument.

sculpt: to carve, mold, or otherwise form material into a particular shape that is three-dimensional.

secure: (v) to tie or fasten firmly.

specs: a short form of the word "spectacles," which are eyeglasses.

thread: (v) to guide some kind of long, thin material, such as thread, string, yarn, or wire, through an opening, which is often very narrow.

tragedy: a serious event that causes sadness or sorrow.

transform: to change the way someone or something looks or acts so the original person or object can no longer be recognized.

tulle: thin, delicate netting made of silk, rayon, or nylon and usually stiffened to make, for example, bridal veils and ballet costumes.

More Books To Read

Come to Percy's Fancy Face Paint Party.
  Annie Kubler (Child's Play International)

Costume Crafts. Worldwide Crafts (series).
  Iain MacLeod-Brudenell (Gareth Stevens)

Disguise. Vivien Kelly (EDC)

Disguises and Fantasy Faces Funstation.
  Christine Edwards and Denise Mountstephens
  (Price Stern Sloan)

Facepaint Fabulous Faces. Demi Brown
  (DK Publishing)

Look What You Can Make with Paper Plates.
  Margie Hayes Richmond (Boyd's Mills Press)

Masks. World Crafts (series). Meryl Doney
  (Franklin Watts)

The Most Excellent Book of Face Painting.
  Margaret Lincoln (Copper Beech Books)

Papier-Mache for Kids. Sheila McGraw
  (Firefly Books)

*The Usborne Book of Masks. How to
  Make* (series). Ray Gibson (EDC)

Videos

Gourd Masks. Native American Crafts (series).
  (Library Video Company)

Making Faces for Halloween. (Quality Video
  and Multimedia, Inc.)

Mask Making. (First Light Video Publishing)

*Maskmaking with Clay. Maskmaking with
  Paper. Art is...* (series). (Crystal Productions)

Masks and Face Coverings. (Crystal Productions)

Simple Mask and Puppet Making.
  (AIMS Multimedia)

Web Sites

www.kidsdomain.com/holiday/earthday/craft/
animalmask.html

users.hsonline.net/kidatart/htdoc/lesson12.htm

Due to the dynamic nature of the Internet, some web sites stay current longer than others. To find
additional web sites, use a reliable search engine with one or more of the following keywords: *clowns,
costumes, crafts, face masks, face painting, makeup, masks,* and *theatrical makeup.*

Index